Overcoming Your Eating Disorder

Overcoming Your Eating Disorder

A Cognitive-Behavioral Therapy Approach for Bulimia Nervosa and Binge-Eating Disorder SECOND EDITION

Workbook

Robin F. Apple • W. Stewart Agras

OXFORD

UNIVERSITY PRESS

2008

OXFORD
UNIVERSITY PRESS

Oxford University Press, Inc., publishes works that further
Oxford University's objective of excellence
in research, scholarship, and education.

Oxford   New York
Auckland   Cape Town   Dar es Salaam   Hong Kong   Karachi
Kuala Lumpur   Madrid   Melbourne   Mexico City   Nairobi
New Delhi   Shanghai   Taipei   Toronto

With offices in
Argentina   Austria   Brazil   Chile   Czech Republic   France   Greece
Guatemala   Hungary   Italy   Japan   Poland   Portugal   Singapore
South Korea   Switzerland   Thailand   Turkey   Ukraine   Vietnam

Copyright © 2008 by Oxford University Press, Inc.

Published by Oxford University Press, Inc.
198 Madison Avenue, New York, New York 10016

www.oup.com

Oxford is a registered trademark of Oxford University Press

ISBN 978-0-19-531168-6 Paper

9 8 7 6 5 4 3 2 1

Printed in the United States of America
on acid-free paper

About Treatments*ThatWork*™

One of the most difficult problems confronting patients with various disorders and diseases is finding the best help available. Everyone is aware of friends or family who have sought treatment from a seemingly reputable practitioner only to find out later from another doctor that the original diagnosis was wrong or the treatments recommended were inappropriate or perhaps even harmful. Most patients, or family members, address this problem by reading everything they can about their symptoms, seeking out information on the Internet, or aggressively "asking around" to tap knowledge from friends and acquaintances. Governments and healthcare policymakers are also aware that people in need don't always get the best treatments—something they refer to as "variability in healthcare practices."

Now healthcare systems around the world are attempting to correct this variability by introducing "evidence-based practice." This simply means that it is in everyone's interest that patients get the most up-to-date and effective care for a particular problem. Healthcare policymakers have also recognized that it is very useful to give consumers of healthcare as much information as possible so that they can make intelligent decisions in a collaborative effort to improve health and mental health. This series, Treatments *ThatWork*™, is designed to accomplish just that. Only the latest and most effective interventions for particular problems are described in user-friendly language. To be included in this series, each treatment program must pass the highest standards of evidence available, as determined by a scientific advisory board. Thus, when individuals suffering from these problems, or their family members, seek an expert clinician who is familiar with these interventions and decide that they are appropriate, they will have confidence that they are receiving the best care available. Of course, only your healthcare professional can decide on the right mix of treatments for you.

If you suffer from bulimia nervosa or binge-eating disorder, this workbook can help. Based on the principles of cognitive-behavioral therapy, the program described will teach you the skills you need to overcome your eating disorder and establish healthy habits. Through daily self-monitoring of your eating patterns, you will learn to regularize your eating and expand the variety of foods you consume. This will help you maintain a healthy weight and will reduce your desire to binge and purge. You will also learn techniques for solving problems, challenging your negative thoughts, and addressing your concerns about weight and shape. Homework exercises and self-assessments reinforce what you learn in sessions with your therapist. At the end of treatment, we fully expect that you will have reduced the number of your binge-eating and purging episodes, improved your body image, and gained a sense of mastery and control over your eating. This program is most effective when carried out in collaboration with your clinician.

David H. Barlow, Editor-in-Chief
Treatments *ThatWork*™
Boston, Massachusetts

Contents

Chapter 1

An Assessment of Your Eating Problems: Is It Time to Begin Treatment?

Goals

- To assess the nature and severity of your eating problems

- To determine if you have an eating disorder

- To learn the facts about bulimia nervosa and binge-eating disorder

- To decide whether this program is right for you

Do You Have an Eating Disorder?

Before you start treatment, it is necessary to assess the extent to which your eating is disordered. You may be uncertain as to whether you simply have peculiar eating habits or have a true eating disorder. You may also feel confused by the wealth of information available about eating disorders. In the early sessions of this program, your therapist will provide feedback about the nature and severity of your eating problems and associated issues. In addition, the following questions will help you begin to understand the nature and seriousness of your eating-related concerns and the extent to which they warrant your involvement in a treatment program of this kind.

- Are you experiencing a loss of control over your eating?

- Do you have recurrent episodes of overeating that you feel are inevitable or that you cannot resist?

- Do you regularly engage in compensatory behaviors, such as purging by means of vomiting, using laxatives, restricting food intake, or exercising excessively?

- Have other interests, activities, or social relationships taken a back seat to your eating and weight-related rituals?

Many people who experience these symptoms have become caught up in a self-perpetuating cycle of disordered eating that includes the following central features:

- An exaggerated sense of the importance of shape and weight

- Episodes of overeating characterized by rapid food consumption when not even hungry to the point of feeling uncomfortably full

- Purging of food through vomiting, use of laxatives, or compulsive exercise

- Negative feelings about body weight and shape

- Fluctuations in self-esteem, based on perceptions of weight and shape

If any of these descriptors apply to you, you may be suffering from *bulimia nervosa* (BN, or bulimia) or a similar disorder called *binge-eating disorder* (BED). Before we describe the characteristics of bulimia nervosa and binge-eating disorder in more detail, we'd like you to read about Sue, a woman who developed an eating disorder in her mid-20s but did not seek treatment for the problem until her late 30s.

Case Study: Sue

- *Sue's story is typical of women with an eating disorder like bulimia nervosa. She was overweight as a child and was raised by an obese adoptive mother who constantly emphasized dieting. Her mother introduced Sue to diet pills and diuretics (water pills) when she was just 11 years old. Sue remembers her mother taunting her by saying she was "too fat to go outside of the house," perhaps in the hope that this would motivate her to diet. Her mother kept the family to a very strict eating pattern of three set meals and one snack per day, including an "enforced" sit-down dinner each night. She also monitored Sue's portions at these meals. Sue mostly remembers feeling like a "zombie," a result of taking diet pills, and did not lose any significant amount of weight.*

She remembers the problem in terms of being overweight, and not in terms of eating-disordered behaviors or attitudes; she was simply given the message that she "should" weigh a lot less.

Over the years, Sue's weight continued to climb despite her mother's early efforts and her own later attempts to diet in various ways. She remembered reaching a weight of 232 lbs (at 5'10") in her mid-20s, around the time she gave birth to her second child. After the birth, she went on a "mission" to lose weight and to "finally become the perfect daughter, wife, and mother." She joined one of the commercial diet programs in the area and started a calorie-controlled plan, along with regular, intense exercise.

All went well with the program until a number of stressful life events occurred, including the illness and eventual death of her mother, who she had been caring for. Around that time, after Sue had already lost nearly 100 lbs by maintaining a very restrictive meal plan, she began to binge eat in response to stress, emotions of any type, and hunger or cravings. At the same time, she started purging by vomiting, abusing laxatives and water pills, fasting, and exercising excessively. When her husband and others noticed that she "looked sick" because of her extreme weight loss and fatigued appearance, Sue agreed to seek treatment for her eating problem and attended regular sessions with a therapist for several months. While she continued to restrict her eating, she was able to give up the laxatives and water pills and exercised less compulsively as a result of the treatment. She generally showed some improvement all around, but these changes lasted for only about a year. Her eating disorder in all respects worsened as she saw her marriage, work, and family life falling apart. And she really hit bottom when she and her husband divorced.

Over the next 12 years, Sue relied on her eating-disordered behaviors to "maintain her goal weight." However, she found it increasingly difficult to maintain that weight because it was too low (126 lbs) for a woman of her height. She reported a great deal of distress because her weight had started to increase over the preceding couple of years, "no matter what she did." When she came to the clinic seeking treatment, her weight was 136 lbs and she reported that she would "feel better" if she could lose a few pounds and also alter her body shape in a way that would lead to a flatter stomach.

She described her dietary regimen as follows. When she was not bingeing, Sue maintained a very rigid pattern of eating. For example, she might eat just one egg white in the morning for many days straight. She might then consider something "normal" for lunch, but only if her children or her new boyfriend persuaded her. Typically, between these skimpy meals that she considered "healthy," Sue engaged in eating episodes that she always characterized as binge eating, no matter what foods or amounts she consumed. Mostly, these episodes involved sweet, high-fat foods that could be eaten quickly, like multiple packages of store-bought chocolate cookies and cartons of frozen yogurt. Between episodes of eating, Sue vomited, spending a portion of the day, if not the entire day, engaged in the behavior of bingeing and purging. As a result of her behavior, Sue had limited energy for physical exercise, an activity that she had come to enjoy. Now she might get out for only a short walk a few times a week. Sue also admitted that much of her free time, when she could be relaxing or enjoying an activity, was caught up in some aspect of her eating disorder (e.g., bingeing and purging or isolating herself from others because she felt fat and depressed).

During the consultation with her therapist, Sue reported a great deal of distress about feeling "caught" in her disordered behaviors and being unable to figure out how to change them without gaining weight. She also noted that over the last couple of years she had become ashamed of herself for succumbing to her eating disorder and not turning it around. She described it as using up more and more of her financial, emotional, and mental resources. As a result, she had begun to feel forced into a style of secretiveness with her friends and significant others, many of whom did not know about her eating disorder. Her life situation had also become so disorganized and chaotic in the past year that she decided to take a medical leave of absence from her position in an administrative job at a small company. She came into treatment worried that, as a result of her eating disorder, she would never get her life back on track. Although she felt quite hopeless, she seemed open to trying nearly anything, including cognitive-behavioral therapy (CBT). ■

Sue suffered from bulimia nervosa, an eating disorder that is estimated to affect 1–3% of young adult women and one tenth that number of men. Bulimia nervosa involves frequent episodes of binge eating, almost always followed by purging and intense feelings of guilt or shame. Bulimics feel out of control during their bingeing episodes. The sense of losing control often involves a reaction to physical and psychological deprivation that results from periods of dietary restriction. Loss of control over eating also appears to consist of conflicting thoughts and feelings about food. Self-deprecating thoughts such as "I don't want to do this," "I have no control over this," or "I'm being a pig again" may accompany a binge. Defiant thoughts such as "I really deserve a treat, so I should eat this ice cream," or "It is going to feel so good to eat exactly what I want" may be a part of the binge as well. The emotional components of a binge may consist of an overwhelming urge to eat, accompanied by positive feelings sometimes described as a "thrill" or as excitement, and negative feelings such as anxiety, anger, guilt, or depression. These feelings and moods of anxiety, anger, or depression often result from unsatisfactory interactions with other people. The most common reason people give for bingeing is a bad mood. Being on a strict diet and feeling hungry and deprived are the next most common reasons given. Binge eating may be an attempt to control or distract from strong feelings.

Most people have the general impression that binge episodes are always very large. In fact, binges can be large or small. Bulimics consume an average of 1,500 calories during a binge, while binge eaters consume an average of 1,000 calories. The calorie range of binges for both types of patients is 100 to 7,000 or more calories. Binges are characterized more by the sensation of losing control over eating than they are by their actual size. Small binges are just as upsetting as large ones. Some evidence suggests that large binges are the first to disappear during successful treatment. Whether or not you define an eating episode as a binge depends on a lot of factors.

Individuals with the most serious eating disorders seem to have the most difficulty appropriately labeling their eating. They demonstrate a tendency to view almost anything they eat as a binge, regardless of the amount they consume. Most people consider an episode of eating a binge if it's accompanied by a sense of being out of control and if they recognize that the behavior is not normal, based on:

■ The time at which it occurs

■ The types and quantities of food consumed at that particular time

■ The location in which they are eating (e.g., in the car, at their desk, or in the library while studying, rather than in the kitchen or dining room)

■ Their eating style (e.g., how fast they eat, if they are standing and eating out of the carton instead of sitting down with a plate of food)

The foods eaten during binges vary widely but typically consist of sweet (often high-fat), easily swallowed foods, such as ice cream, cookies, breads, cereals, and so on. Some binges consist of several servings of a main course or double or triple helpings of all courses of a meal. Bulimia is characterized by repeated binges and bouts of purging intended to compensate for the excess calories consumed. Patients with bulimia nervosa often drink large quantities of fluids to make vomiting easier.

The relationship between binges and purges is complex. The size or contents of a binge or the quantity of fluids consumed may be deliberately increased to make self-induced vomiting easier. On the other hand, once a bulimic decides that she will purge, she may "release" herself from her usual eating-related constraints and increase the amount of food she is willing to eat. She may eat "everything she wants" because she knows she is just going to purge later anyway. What tends to happen over time is that, once purging begins, the size and frequency of binge episodes increases. In addition to vomiting, purging can include using laxatives and laxative teas, diuretics, or water pills, and exercising excessively. Some people will impose a starvation diet on themselves or fast for a day or more at a time after they binge. They do this to offset all the calories they consumed. Occasionally, bulimics will chew their food and then spit it out either into their hands, a napkin, the sink, or some other place.

On average, a person starts becoming a bulimic or a binge eater at the age of 19. Purging usually begins a few months after the onset of bulimia, and gradual weight gain is seen in binge eaters after approximately the same amount of time. However, about 10% of bulimics are overweight, while some 25–30% have had a history of anorexia nervosa. Between 20 and 30% of patients with binge-eating disorder have purged in the past, often meeting criteria for bulimia nervosa at that time. Others have tried to purge but find that they cannot do it. Some find it repulsive. To meet formal diagnostic criteria for bulimia nervosa, a person must binge at least twice a week for three months. Other features of bulimia nervosa include being preoccupied with shape and weight and overly critical of one's body image, and having exaggerated concerns about the potential for weight gain, despite maintaining a weight within the normal range.

The eating disorder anorexia nervosa (with binge eating and purging) has features in common with bulimia nervosa. However, to be diagnosed as an anorexic, a person must weigh at least 15% less than the normal standard. If you believe you are suffering from anorexia nervosa, your lowered weight and nutritional status may place you at higher risk for certain medical complications (for example, loss of your menstrual cycle). While you might benefit from the treatment method described in this workbook, you should discuss the implications of your diagnosis with your therapist and primary care physician before starting this program. Certainly, the program would be useful to you, but only if you simultaneously make a commitment to gradually gain enough weight to return to the normal range for your height.

If you are binge eating without purging, you may be experiencing binge-eating disorder. Binge-eating disorder is different from bulimia nervosa in that binge eaters don't usually purge, and they are often overweight or obese. Also, to obtain a diagnosis of BED, a person must have engaged in the behavior for longer than three months. When appropriate, this workbook will include special "For the Binge-Eating Patient" sections that address issues particular to BED and/or to overweight bulimics. Although most of the interventions for BED and bulimia are similar, there are a couple of differences. First, the factors that contribute to binges for individuals with BED are different from the factors for bulimics. Unlike bulimics, binge eaters do not necessarily binge because they are hungry. However, both bulimics and binge eaters share other characteristics, like low self-esteem, negative moods, charged interpersonal interactions, and concerns about weight and shape. A model depicting how these factors interact is shown in Chapter 4. Binge eaters seem to suffer from a fairly chronic loss of control or restraint over their eating, which causes them to engage in frequent snacking or "grazing" behaviors. The foundation of problematic eating patterns in those who are bulimic is often a very strict diet that they can't stick to because it is unrealistic. This causes them to overeat in a binge when they lose restraint.

The differences in the two conditions do have implications for treatment. Although adopting a regularized eating pattern that consists of three meals and two snacks per day has proven beneficial for both bulimics and binge eaters, the treatments for the two disorders differ with respect to the level of restraint or control that is recommended. While it is important for bulimics and binge eaters to adopt a "flexible" approach to meal planning, binge eaters are encouraged to become more deliberate about planning, structuring, and controlling their eating times and the types and portions of food they eat, and to commit to regular exercise. Bulimics, on the other hand are encouraged to use flexible guidelines to loosen their rules and become less rigid by, for example, allowing themselves to eat breakfast or other meals that were typically skipped, adding formerly "feared" or "avoided" foods into their meal plan regularly, and allowing for days off from exercise. Binge eaters are encouraged from the very start of the program to adopt a "heart-smart" approach in choosing food. It is important for binge eaters to decrease the amount of fat they eat to less than approximately 30% of their total calories (along the lines of the recommendations made by the American Heart Association), to limit portion sizes, and to implement an exercise regimen equivalent to at least 30 minutes per day of brisk walking. Although some similar recommendations may be made for the overweight bulimic, these will be included at a later point in the treatment, only after the target behaviors of binge eating and purging have been interrupted through normalization of the meal pattern.

Case Study: Barbra

Barbra, a successful ad executive in her mid-30s and mother of three children, had a history of weight and eating issues dating back to her adolescence, stemming in part from her upbringing in a high-achieving, appearance-oriented family. As she grew up, her mother was often dieting and encouraged her daughter, who was then only 10 or so pounds overweight, to join her in this endeavor. As a result, Barbra felt a chronic sense of shame about her body weight and shape and much pressure to diet, even though by and large she was within or close to the normal weight range for her height. When she came to the clinic seeking help, she described her problem as "having lost control over eating." She described a years-long pattern of becoming "really excited" about starting a new diet approach, whether a commercial program, fad diet, or self-imposed plan, typically along with an exercise regimen, which she might sustain for up to a few weeks, during which time she might lose a few pounds (typically just 5–10). Then, as quickly as she became excited about her new diet, she would lose interest in it altogether when she "cheated" on the diet and overindulged. One instance of breaking the rules of her diet was all it took to make Barbra start binge eating again. For example, Barbra would start most mornings vowing to "be good" by eating something reasonable for breakfast, such as eggs or some cereal or a breakfast bar, but at some point during the day, often as early as mid-morning, she would confront "bad" foods, eat "too much" of them, and "decide" that the day was shot anyway, so she might as well continue to overeat.

What often set her off were foods available in her workplace, such as bowls of small candies on the desks of her coworkers, pastries or cakes brought in for a special occasion, or a catered lunch for the office. Occasionally, the "good day" would extend until the evening hours. In those situations, Barbra would limit her mid-morning snacks, order a healthy lunch, such as a salad or sandwich, and possibly stay in control through some or most of the afternoon or into the evening. But usually something would get in the way of this healthy eating pattern and she would begin overeating at some point. She and her husband shared the responsibility of picking up healthy takeout food for the family, but Barbra often refused to eat with them and then would overeat later or the next day. If she did eat a normal, healthy dinner, Barbra might continue eating into the evening hours, consuming desserts and/or snacks. Very occasionally, usually when she had skipped meals during the day, she awoke in the middle of the night and had a snack.

In addition to the foods that triggered Barbra's overeating episodes, the combined stresses of a high-profile full-time job, married life, and raising kids contributed a great deal to her relationship with food. In some respects, food had become Barbra's number one way to reduce stress, although she grew to realize that often it created more stress for her than it relieved. For example, Barbra's views of herself swung radically, depending on whether or not she felt "thin" or "fat" (her weight did frequently fluctuate 15–20 lbs, depending on her dieting) or in or out of control of her eating. Her husband had grown very dissatisfied with their intimate life because she was unwilling to have sex when she had overeaten or felt overweight. Barbra spent so much time worrying about her weight, attempting solutions for her weight and eating problem, hiding her overeating, exercising, and hiding in shame when she felt fat that she neglected her friends, her children, and her husband. She gave as much as she could at her office, but she acknowledged that even her professional performance had likely suffered from her eating disorder and weight concerns. As a result, Barbra admitted feeling depressed at times, although this was clearly secondary to her problems with eating and weight.

When she began treatment, Barbra's primary goal was to "lose weight," until she was reminded that effective treatment for her binge-eating disorder required that she first stabilize her eating behaviors. After regularizing her eating, she could then work toward a slow and steady weight loss. At 5'2" and 145 lbs, it was reasonable for Barbra to consider gradual weight loss, and she was able to consider, in reviewing the CBT model of her disorder, the relationship between normalizing her eating patterns and losing weight in this fashion, slowly, over time. She initially took to the CBT formulation and tools. She monitored her eating habits regularly by keeping food records but had a hard time with portion control (finding it easier to skip meals or restrict or grossly overeat or binge rather than eat in moderation) and found it difficult to weigh herself only once a week. Over time, her eating habits did stabilize, and she became more comfortable adhering to the regular meal pattern, but she persisted through the course of treatment in wanting to lose weight into the 130 or so range. Particularly because there was a family celebration coming up a few months after treatment was to end, Barbra was considered to be at high risk for resuming some of the more extreme dieting behaviors that had contributed to her eating and weight problem in the first place. ■

Some studies suggest that bulimia nervosa tends to run in families. Twin studies suggest that bulimia nervosa is genetic and inheritable, although the exact nature of what is inherited remains unknown. Other studies suggest that individuals with bulimia may have lower levels of serotonin than do people without the disorder and that bingeing on high-carbohydrate foods tends to alleviate the condition. Serotonin is a chemical in the brain that regulates mood, emotion, sleep, and appetite. Low serotonin levels may also be associated with depression, a frequent accompaniment of bulimia.

Environmental factors may also lead to bulimia. The pressure on women to be thin has increased in the last 25 years. This appears to be due to a portrayal of ever thinner ideal body types in the media, combined with a rise in the popularity of commercial diet programs of various types. Other factors that may contribute to bulimia nervosa include having a family history of obesity, being teased about weight and shape by peers during adolescence, and having low self-esteem.

Many individuals, like Sue, develop bulimia nervosa while trying to diet or after a period of actual or attempted weight loss. They report that when they first discover purging it gives them an incredible sense of control over their eating, weight, and shape. But eventually, the behavior begins to control them because more time, energy, and money are taken up by the eating disorder. For example, they may put money aside specifically to buy foods they can binge on and items to help them purge, like laxatives and water pills. In addition, individuals may schedule their work, social engagements, and other tasks around their bingeing and purging episodes. They may even avoid friends and loved ones who may be suspicious of their behavior. To the extent that binge eating and purging become habit and replace other, more meaningful activities, bulimics often describe their eating disorder as "taking on a life of its own" and more or less taking over *their* life. The sense of shame and guilt associated with repetitively engaging in secret behaviors that they consider "disgusting" may contribute also to progressive social withdrawal and increasing depression. Even as bulimics may commonly acknowledge feeling distressed about a lifestyle that has grown increasingly isolated and constricted, they may not have the motivation to reestablish a range of activities and relationships. Indeed, many bulimics report that they feel chronically anxious and exhausted and see any new undertaking as being "too hard" and also as less likely to make them feel as good as they do when they are bingeing and purging. In extreme cases, patients have said, "All I want to do is stay home, eat, and throw up."

Development of Sue's Eating Disorder

When Sue started treatment, she wanted to learn more about all aspects of her eating disorder: why and when it had developed and for what reasons it had become a significant problem for her. Like others with eating problems similar to hers, Sue had had, from a young age, the factors that predispose a person to develop bulimia. These included having had a somewhat "moody," shy, and sensitive temperament; having been overweight during childhood; and having had an overweight mother who judged her for being "fat" and who imposed rigid eating patterns and diet programs on her, including diet pills. As an adoptee, Sue also had an early, although unremembered, experience of abandonment. When combined, these experiences had a significant effect on Sue's body image. Because she felt bad about herself for being heavy, she was more likely to resort to drastic measures in an attempt to lose weight. However, Sue led an active social life, dated regularly, and married at the age of 20. But once she settled into married life and gave birth to two children (one at the age of 20, and the other at the age of 25), Sue's weight problem increasingly bothered her. She began to feel unattractive as a wife and embarrassed for her children, whose friends had more slender and active mothers. She also felt ashamed about her weight. It was following the birth of her second child that she started to engage in very extreme efforts to lose weight, joining a commercial diet program and beginning rigorous exercise. At that point in Sue's life, weight loss meant nothing short of "perfection" for her, even if it cost her considerably (e.g., by triggering a very serious eating disorder).

The behaviors that resulted because of Sue's increasing discomfort with her weight and body were predictable. She restricted her food intake, consistent with the diet program's requirements, regularly followed a strenuous regimen of exercise, and began to lose weight at an alarming rate, not without the aid of water pills and purging, which she started some months into her diet, when her weight loss had slowed. After several months, she had lost 50 lbs, then 80; eventually, her total weight loss would exceed 100 lbs. It was at some point during this period that Sue's husband told her that she "looked awful and needed help." This prompted Sue to enter treatment for the first time. By that time, Sue was quite entrenched in a vicious cycle of restricting her food intake, binge eating, and purging (by vomiting and over-exercising), and taking water pills and fasting. While using these strategies, her thoughts and feelings about herself, her body image, and her relationships became more and more erratic and negative, rather than improving as she had hoped they would with weight loss. She began to pull away from others more than she ever had before, when "feeling fat," or when engrossed in the behaviors of her eating disorder. She made herself only marginally available to others when she was dieting strictly. Understandably, her family members found these behaviors exasperating. By her own admission, Sue was incredibly frustrated with herself for staying so "stuck" in the cycle of her eating disorder and feeling even worse about her body than she did before the eating disorder began—when she was simply "stuck" with the problem of being overweight.

Like Sue, bulimics consistently find deterioration in their thought processes, emotions, and behaviors as their disorder worsens. They are easily distracted and preoccupied with particular aspects of their eating behavior (e.g., what, when, and how much they eat) and specific worries about their body shape or weight. Often, they ignore other real-life concerns and relationships with significant others. Because of the "addictive" nature of the behavior, bulimics may focus almost all their attention on working out the logistics and mechanics of bingeing and purging so that no one will know what they're doing. As a result, the bulimic individual may begin to feel shameful and deceptive, while those around her may perceive her as chronically secretive, preoccupied, and distracted. Bulimia also takes a toll on an individual's understanding of herself, her interests, her motivations, and her priorities, goals, and emotions. Labels for emotional states may be limited to "hungry, full, fat, or thin," or "bad or good," all depending on where in the cycle of binge eating, purging, weight loss, or weight gain the person is. As more and more time is spent in the behaviors of the eating disorder, the bulimic individual may simply give up on engaging in more meaningful activities and relationships, to the point of losing the ability to interact effectively in the world. She may even forget which types of activities and relationships are joyful and fulfilling. Feelings of ineffectiveness and "loss of control" may permeate many experiences not even associated with weight or eating. This may be a result of the bulimic's not being able to effectively solve problems in multiple areas of her life. For too long, she has relied on food-related behaviors to cope with problems. Bulimics also feel ineffective because of repeated, unsuccessful attempts at dieting, which only lead to more binge eating. Strict dieting is often viewed as the only effective means for overcoming binge eating and potential weight gain. Dieting failures may result in fear, hopelessness, and despair that weight and eating problems can never be overcome. Psychological conditions that may co-occur with bulimia include depression, anxiety, and substance or alcohol abuse. It can be especially difficult for bulimics to stop their behavior because it brings them certain benefits. For example, bingeing and purging may temporarily improve mood and eliminate negative feelings. It also helps individuals avoid unpleasant situations in that it creates reasons for them to escape or avoid the various challenges and responsibilities of life. Bingeing and purging may also create a relaxed and calm sensation, and many bulimics come to rely on this sensation as their primary coping tool.

Bulimia and Binge-Eating Disorder Checklist

1. Do you engage in recurrent episodes of overeating during which you feel a loss of control and consume a lot more food than average in a limited period of time?

    Yes _____   No _____

2. Do you regularly engage in vomiting or another form of purging behavior (such as using laxatives, diuretics, enemas, compulsive exercise, or fasting) to compensate for the excess caloric intake?

    Yes _____   No _____

3. Are you preoccupied with concerns about your shape and weight?

Yes _____   No _____

Is This Program Right for You?

This therapy program was developed to treat bulimia nervosa and related conditions such as binge-eating disorder. If you answered yes to all the preceding questions, then it is likely you have bulimia nervosa. If you answered yes to questions 1 and 3 only, it is likely you have binge-eating disorder. Whether you struggle with BN or BED, you are likely to see an improvement in your symptoms if you make a commitment to follow this program. Before moving on, however, take some time to consider the following issues.

Mixed Feelings About Starting Treatment

It is natural to experience mixed feelings as you consider starting this treatment program. Working to change a long-standing behavior pattern can be difficult. As previously stated, obviously there are rewarding aspects of your behavior, or you wouldn't have come to rely on it habitually to cope. It is crucial that you embrace your mixed feelings about beginning this program. Examine not only all that you might *gain* but also all that you might *lose* in making the decision to give up your eating disorder. For example, the "costs" of treatment include investments in time, money, and emotional energy, and the lost opportunities to pursue other activities that might conflict with your program. To manage these obstacles to treatment maturely and effectively, it is important that you face them head on. Many individuals experience one or more "false starts," making a decision to begin treatment but then postponing or showing up to sessions only now and then, or not showing up at all. We encourage you to make a heart- and gut-felt decision based on all the factors discussed so that you can guarantee a positive experience for yourself. The Costs and Benefits Analysis worksheet on page 21 will help you with your decision.

Motivation

We find that the patients who do best in focused treatment programs begin when they are able to focus their full attention on their recovery and make it a top priority in their life. Although a strong commitment to therapy does not require withdrawing from other real-life commitments such as personal relationships and work, it may involve postponing other "elective" activities (for example, extended travel to a faraway place) until the treatment is well under way. If you cannot make that kind of commitment now, we recommend that you postpone starting the program until you can. We make this strong recommendation for the simple reason that if you do focus and commit yourself fully, you are very likely to succeed! However, if you are distracted and only partially engaged, treatment is far less likely to be successful for you and will then taint any subsequent efforts to use this program.

The Willingness to Change

Another aspect of motivation involves the willingness to change old ways of thinking, feeling, and behaving. We ask that you develop an attitude of experimentation and "risk taking." We want you to test out new strategies, even if they seem rather strange, uncomfortable, or counterintuitive at first. Success in this program means taking a "leap of faith," trusting that if you learn and apply the methods presented here you will have a good chance of overcoming your eating disorder. Maintaining the spirit of adventure can help you stick with the program even when the process gets tough and success seems very far away.

One issue that can frustrate and confuse even the most devoted and hardworking of patients is the prospect of weight gain during treatment, an issue that will be covered in much more detail in a later chapter. Although we cannot predict the effects of the treatment program on *your* weight, the results of CBT treatments like the program offered here, compiled over years of working with eating-disordered patients with issues like yours, suggest that on average there may be a weight gain of up to 4 lbs. This is especially typical of patients who start the program at a weight that is below average for their height. The weight gain in these individuals usually represents a return to a healthier weight range. Patients who make an internal commitment to accepting that their body weight will stabilize where it *should* be are the most likely to follow through with the interventions presented to them during treatment and are ultimately the most successful in the program.

Simultaneous Treatments

This program seems to work best when it is used in the context of a therapy relationship focused exclusively on treating the eating disorder, whether it be bulimia nervosa or binge-eating disorder. It is most effective when it is offered as a discrete treatment program, rather than combined with, or added to, an ongoing therapy addressing different issues. In other words, patients are best able to make use of the program when not simultaneously involved in other psychotherapies. This reduces the possibility of confusion.

Medications

A variety of medications, primarily antidepressants like Prozac, have been used to treat bulimia nervosa, typically as an add-on to psychotherapy. Although these medications appear to have some therapeutic benefits in some individuals, typically by reducing appetite or the urge to overeat or binge or by enhancing mood, these effects may diminish over time. They may also mask the problems, preventing the individual from learning and practicing the skills required for permanent change. We recommend that you discuss the issue of medication with your therapist as you begin treatment. No matter what you decide regarding medications at the outset of treatment, you may want to reconsider medications at some later date, depending on your response to this program.

The Complication of Being Overweight

We know that approximately 10% of bulimic patients (and many more binge-eating patients) are overweight and that binge eating is considered the most significant behavioral contribution to weight gain. Because the primary emphasis of this program is to overcome binge eating and *not necessarily* to lose weight, the program is best considered an *indirect* route to eventual weight loss. Again, this is true *only* for those who are overweight by clinical standards when they start the program. Given that the cognitive-behavioral model for BN and BED shows that dieting is one of the most significant causes of binge eating, intentional dieting is not recommended. Rather, program participants are asked to put their goals for losing weight on hold and to focus instead on the behaviors that will make it easy to maintain weight and, over time, possibly lead to gradual weight loss, if necessary. These behaviors include establishing a regular pattern of meals and snacks that does not include binge eating or strict dieting, and addressing all the other behaviors, thoughts, and feelings that might get in the way of that healthy pattern. For binge eaters and overweight bulimics, behaviors will also include decreasing fat intake and increasing exercise. Patients who start the program overweight must make a commitment to changing the behaviors that contribute most to their disordered eating habits first. They need to understand that weight loss might be an eventual possibility but not necessarily a probable outcome of making all the recommended behavior changes.

Other Emotional Problems

Eating problems such as bulimia nervosa and binge-eating disorder often occur in conjunction with other conditions, such as depression, anxiety, and/or substance abuse. When alcohol and/or drug abuse or dependence or severe depression or anxiety coexist with bulimia nervosa or binge-eating disorder, it is usually best to treat these issues before beginning treatment for an eating disorder. These issues could interfere with your ability to adhere to the recommendations made during the treatment for your eating disorder, or the conditions might worsen in response to the rigors of this program.

Treatment Benefits

What can you expect to gain from treatment? If you follow the program carefully, you should experience a significant improvement in the behaviors and attitudes most central to your eating disorder. These include a reduction in dietary restriction and the number of your binge-eating and purging episodes, an improvement in your body image, and an increased sense of mastery over eating.

But in anticipating your response to treatment, you need to consider the following. You must be able to give treatment a high priority in your life for several months. If there are other major life issues or changes in your life that might interfere with your treatment, you should discuss these in detail with your therapist. If necessary, you should consider waiting to begin treatment until these issues are resolved. Also, you must be motivated to follow through with all the behavior-change recommendations suggested to you. Although it is sometimes difficult to effect these changes, the recommendations are based on research that has demonstrated their effectiveness in helping patients overcome eating disorders. You will only be selling yourself and your treatment short if you "cut corners" or attempt in any way not to fully take on the challenges of this program. Finally, the treatment will likely work best if you accept in advance that it is going to be difficult, requiring much hard work and determination on your part. You also need to rely on your therapist and put your trust in him or her. If you are willing to make this type of wholehearted commitment to the program, we are convinced the program will be effective in helping you overcome your eating disorder.

The Effectiveness of Cognitive-Behavioral Therapy

You should know that cognitive-behavioral therapy has been tested in numerous controlled studies and, when compared with a number of other approaches, has been found to be the most effective approach to the treatment of bulimia nervosa and binge-eating disorder. During treatment, about 50–55% of patients completely recover, and a further 25% show very good improvement. Some of this 25% will completely recover over the next few months if they continue to apply the principles learned during therapy. You should be optimistic about this treatment and the strong likelihood that it will improve your eating disorder. Also, the results of cognitive-behavioral therapy appear to be long lasting. Follow-up studies suggest that most patients maintain their improvements after completing therapy. Although some patients may experience an occasional increase in their symptoms, particularly during times of stress, re-implementing the strategies learned during treatment and/or returning for a few extra therapy sessions to quickly address the issues and overcome the lapse are effective strategies.

Because overweight or obesity can accompany binge-eating disorder (and may in some cases accompany bulimia nervosa), weight-loss treatment may be useful following successful completion of cognitive-behavioral therapy. It has been shown that patients who stop binge eating are able to lose a modest amount of weight during therapy and to maintain that weight loss for a year post-treatment. In contrast, patients who do not stop binge eating gain weight during both the treatment and follow-up periods. It seems likely that cognitive-behavioral therapy combined with a modest weight-loss program allows the overweight binge eater or bulimic to achieve small but useful weight losses without the consequences of dietary restraint.

At this time, it may be helpful for you to complete a cost–benefit analysis regarding the decision to begin treatment now. Take a few moments to complete the worksheet provided here.

Making a Decision About Treatment

By now you should have a developed a reasonable level of understanding about your eating problems and your readiness, appropriateness, and motivation for this program of treatment. The decision tree shown in Figure 1.1 should help you determine whether or not to begin treatment at this time.

Beginning Therapy

Deciding to begin cognitive-behavioral therapy treatment for your eating disorder is no small thing. It is a decision that warrants much thoughtful consideration, even if you haven't thought much about it and were prepared to forge ahead and start treatment without much deliberation. We hope this chapter has helped you with the various aspects of your decision-making process.

Costs and Benefits Analysis

	Costs	Benefits
Costs and Benefits of Beginning Treatment		
Costs and Benefits of Not Beginning Treatment		

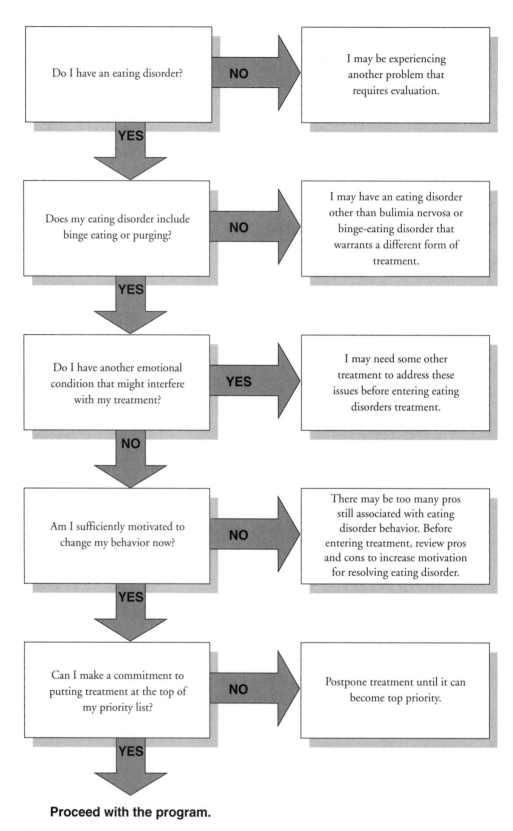

Proceed with the program.

Figure 1.1 Decision Tree

We believe that you will find the treatment program and this workbook helpful and user-friendly. This CBT treatment program represents a state-of-the-art approach that can be helpful to both those with bulimia nervosa and those with binge-eating disorder. As previously discussed, you are participating in a therapy with demonstrated effectiveness across a number of controlled-research studies.

Compared to more traditional psychotherapies you might have heard about that mostly involve talking, expressing emotions, and eliciting helpful, general feedback from your therapist, CBT requires that you approach your therapy with a spirit of adventure and experimentation. You will actively engage in goal setting, including completing homework assignments that will enable you to test a range of new behaviors, thoughts, attitudes, and feelings, which may at first feel uncomfortable or scary. The collaborative relationship you will establish with your therapist is also somewhat different in nature from these relationships in more traditional therapies. Your therapist will provide a supportive, encouraging, and reassuring foundation to facilitate your change process, but ultimately it is up to you to agree wholeheartedly to "experiment" by exposing yourself to the types of "risky" new behaviors and attitudes that have been proven over time to help others like you overcome their eating disorders. We understand that it can be very difficult to change long-standing habits related to an eating disorder. However, based on our many years of experience treating individuals with eating disorders, we believe that the techniques introduced here will prove extremely helpful to you in your attempts to overcome problems with binge eating and purging.

As emphasized earlier, deciding whether or not to begin CBT for your eating disorder is no small task. You and your therapist might spend a considerable amount of time talking about various issues before you choose to start treatment. Typically, this decision takes a few (2–4) or even several (6–8) sessions and relies on your own assessment of your eating problems and also your therapist's input. No matter when the decision is made, the two of you will talk at length about the pros and cons of starting CBT at this point, as opposed to delaying treatment, opting for another form of treatment, or not starting treatment at all. If you decide to forgo treatment for now, your therapist will help you identify a number of other treatment options that may be available to you.

If you decide to begin the program now, you should know that this workbook will play an integral role. It provides a "take-home" component that can help you prepare for treatment and allows you to review the content of each of your sessions. It also includes various worksheets and forms you can use to track your progress. The workbook is structured, sequentially arranged, and also flexible. It directly corresponds to the therapist guide used to conduct your treatment. It is to your advantage to prepare for your sessions in advance by previewing the relevant chapter(s), based on the issues you and your therapist discussed in the last session, and using the workbook after each session to review the issues that were addressed in the session. The workbook can also serve as a tool to help you educate significant others and friends about your eating problems and current treatment, and it will be yours to keep for reference and review once you have completed the program. A note about gender: Because eating disorders such as bulimia nervosa and binge-eating disorder are much more prevalent in girls and women than in boys and men, some of the issues will be discussed more from the female perspective than from the male point of view, although we do recognize the presence and significance of these issues for men.

Homework

✎ Use the Bulimia and Binge-Eating Disorder Checklist in the text above to determine whether or not you have an eating disorder.

✎ Complete the Costs and Benefits Analysis sheet and examine your readiness for treatment.

✎ Talk with your therapist about the advisability of beginning treatment at this time.

Self-Assessment

Take some time to review the content of this chapter and complete the following self-assessment. Answer by filling in the correct words or phrases, or by circling T (True) or F (False). Answers can be found in the Appendix.

1.   Name four of the central features of bulimia nervosa or binge-eating disorder.

2.   Binge-eating episodes can be large or small, as long as the eating is experienced as out of control.   T   F

3.   Name some of the factors that may contribute to the development of bulimia.

4.   Name some of the factors that may get in the way of your starting or following through with the treatment program.

5.   What is the difference between bulimia nervosa and binge-eating disorder?

6. This program is appropriate for the treatment of
   bulimia nervosa only.   T   F

7. What can you expect to get out of the program?

   _____

   _____

   _____

   _____

Chapter 2

What Can You Expect from the Program?

Goals

- To understand this program and what it will involve

- To learn about this workbook

Review of Previous Chapter

Chapter 1 presented an overview of the features of bulimia nervosa and binge-eating disorder. You should have been able to use the information from this chapter to assess the nature and severity of your eating problems and the appropriateness of this program at this point.

Overview

Before beginning any therapy program, you should know what to expect. This chapter provides an introduction to the CBT program and an overview of the workbook. It also outlines the three phases of treatment, the structure and content of individual therapy sessions, the types of questions you'll be asked in the first session, and instructions for using this workbook.

Whether or not this is your first time in therapy, you can expect that this experience will be useful and memorable. You will learn a lot about yourself and the thoughts, feelings, and behaviors that are connected in various ways to your eating disorder. Let us spend some time discussing the details of this treatment program.

In the first consultation session with your therapist, he or she will want to spend some time getting to know you better, hearing your "story," and taking your history. This discussion might take the form of a semi-structured interview to maintain a focus on the general nature of your eating disorder, such as the degree to which binge eating, dietary restriction, purging, and weight concerns might be present. Your therapist will also ask you questions about when, how, and why your eating disorder first developed when it did, and what factors have contributed to its getting better or worse from time to time. Your current patterns of eating (and also exercising and purging, when relevant) will also be discussed to understand the triggers for specific episodes of the problem behavior. In addition, your therapist will ask you about the details of these episodes, including the specific thoughts and feelings you had before, during, and after; the extent to which you might restrict your eating in other instances; the existence of food-related rules; and the nature of your concerns about body weight and shape. You will also be asked about any prior therapy experiences—what was helpful, what wasn't, and why or why not—and what you are expecting and hoping for in making a commitment to participate in this program. Your therapist will examine your pattern of purging in detail, including a history of the various methods you have used (e.g., vomiting, using laxatives or water pills) or are using. You will be asked about other issues that are sometimes related to eating disorders, such as your moods, that is, whether depression or anxiety have been problematic, and your use of alcohol and/or drugs. Finally, you will be asked some questions about your medical history and that of your family, and your relationships with family members, significant others, and friends. At the end of this session, there will be time for you to discuss your degree of motivation and commitment to follow through with this treatment now that you have learned a bit more about it. At this point, you will also be asked to review your life circumstances, including any obstacles that might stand in the way of your fully committing yourself to therapy and following it through to the end. If obstacles are found, you and your therapist will spend some time discussing the pros and cons of beginning treatment at this time, and together you will make a decision about whether or not to proceed as planned.

The Cognitive-Behavioral Model of Bulimia Nervosa and Binge-Eating Disorder

This treatment program is based on a cognitive-behavioral model (described in more detail in Chapter 4) for understanding the factors that contribute to the onset and the maintenance of bulimia nervosa and binge-eating disorder. The model assumes there is a relationship among dietary restriction, negative mood, low self-esteem, and binge-eating and purging behaviors. Although there are individual differences, most patients with bulimia nervosa and binge-eating disorder have histories compatible with this model. Once he or she obtains your history, your therapist will map out the elements of the model on paper for you. Each phase of this program is geared toward correcting some aspect of your eating problem that reflects a part of the model (such as certain problem behaviors and attitudes) and thereby contributes to the cycle of binge eating and purging.

Rationale for Cognitive-Behavioral Therapy

The first aim of treatment is to help you regularize your eating patterns. The goal is to work toward a routine of eating "by the clock," consuming three meals and two snacks per day at regular intervals. Because of your eating disorder, your body no longer knows when it is truly full or truly hungry. It gives you false signals. This is why it is so important to establish consistent eating habits. Your therapist will make it clear that you are expected to make this change gradually. It is essential for you to take some risks, however. Therapy is an excellent time to experiment with new behaviors, to observe the results of those behavior changes, and to make use of the opportunity to obtain feedback and guidance from your therapist. Although you may have initial reservations about establishing a regular pattern of eating because you may fear you will gain weight, it has been proven that CBT patients gain only a few pounds. Most of this is water weight, a result of your body's trying to overcome its dehydrated state. This issue will be addressed in more detail in a future session.

After taking your complete history, your therapist will describe this workbook and provide more details about the program.

Even if you have previously been in therapy for your eating disorder, you may not have used a workbook to guide your therapy. The workbook is intended for individuals with bulimia nervosa or binge-eating disorder to use under the supervision of a qualified professional. It is not intended for use as a self-help manual. As you already know from reading Chapter 1, the workbook contains background information that will improve your understanding of bulimia nervosa, binge-eating disorder, and the cognitive-behavioral approach to treatment. Each chapter contains important educational material, relevant exercises, homework assignments, and self-assessments. In general, you should plan on proceeding at a pace of approximately one chapter per session. However, because they set the stage for the remainder of therapy, the first four chapters are particularly important, and it is worthwhile to read and review each of them several times during the first two weeks of treatment.

There are many benefits associated with using a workbook. First, the structure, although flexible, ensures that the treatment procedures are optimally sequenced and that all the components of therapy are adequately covered. For example, your therapy program will begin with a focus on organizing your eating patterns. Once you've developed a regular eating pattern, you will move on to subsequent issues, such as introducing feared foods into your diet and learning how to problem solve. You and your therapist will determine the pace for moving through the workbook, based on the particulars of your eating disorder and your rate of progress. Second, the workbook functions to keep both you and your therapist on track. Without the benefit of a workbook, it can be easy to devote a considerable amount of therapy time to issues that are not central to helping you overcome your eating disorder. Third, the procedures described in this workbook have been tested and proven effective in controlled, treatment-outcome research studies.

There are additional benefits associated with using a workbook. One advantage is that it provides a constant source of educational material and motivational support relating to your therapy. In addition, you will read the workbook ahead of each session, better preparing yourself for what is to come. You can also refresh your memory concerning the material and procedures covered in past sessions by reviewing relevant chapters. The workbook also serves as a reference and guide after treatment has ended as you work to maintain and build upon the gains you've made. Finally, you may want to use the workbook as a vehicle to initiate discussions with significant others about your eating disorder and this treatment program.

A Note About Self-Disclosure

A few years ago, it was usual for patients with bulimia nervosa to hide their binge eating and purging from those with whom they lived. This situation has changed somewhat as eating disorders have become better accepted because of education through public awareness. However, some individuals with eating disorders continue to hide their behavior from everyone. It may be useful for you to consider the extent to which you have thus far confided in anyone about your eating disorder. If you have not disclosed it to significant others, such as a spouse or partner, it will be helpful to explore this with your therapist and to talk about the advantages and disadvantages of keeping the problem to yourself. Revealing your disorder to those who are close to you can give you extra motivation to improve because your eating disorder becomes more real. In addition, opening up to others about your eating problem may relieve some of the burden of guilt, and the necessity for deceiving those with whom you live by hiding the evidence of binge eating and purging. Using this workbook to educate significant others about your eating disorder can facilitate self-disclosure.

Structure of Treatment

The therapy is intended to last 18–20 sessions spread over a six-month period. Individual sessions are usually 50 minutes long. We have found it helpful to schedule more frequent sessions in the beginning of treatment, for example, two sessions per week for each of the first two weeks, followed by weekly sessions until the last three meetings, which are held at two-week intervals. The more frequent early sessions represent a "higher dose" of therapy that provides you and your therapist an opportunity to quickly come to grips with the problem.

It may also help jump-start the process of behavior change so that you can very quickly experience the benefits. The purpose of the longer interval between sessions toward the end of treatment is to give you more time to experiment with your newly learned eating behaviors and attitudes, test your skills at working through any problems that might arise, and anticipate potential obstacles to maintaining your progress after treatment.

The program is divided into three distinct but overlapping phases, focusing on changing behavior, understanding binge triggers, and preventing relapses. The length of each phase and the degree of overlap between one phase and another is determined by you and your therapist, depending on your rate of progress and the nature of your eating disorder. Although you may not need the full therapy program, your therapist will cover the essential elements of each phase.

Phase 1: Behavior Change

Although it is not mandatory, completing the first four sessions of this program in a 2-week period helps establish a satisfactory working relationship between you and your therapist and provides you with an opportunity to rapidly respond to treatment. The first goal of Phase 1 is to teach you how to self-monitor in order to clarify the details of your eating habits. You will use Daily Food Records to record your food intake. Your therapist will use the data from these records to show how the CBT model of binge eating applies to you. The main element of the CBT model is that restricting your diet leads to excessive hunger and eventually to loss of control over your eating, resulting in episodes of binge eating (see Chapter 4 for a model illustrating this cycle). For the patient with bulimia nervosa, this leads to purging and guilt, and lowers self-esteem. For the patient with binge-eating disorder, the excess calories consumed while binge eating cause weight gain, leading to increased concern about weight and shape, and guilt about gaining weight. To overcome this pattern of eating, you will be encouraged to eat three meals and two snacks a day at regular intervals (eating by the clock). You will also be educated about weight and asked to weigh yourself weekly. Formal problem solving is often introduced in this phase to help you overcome specific problems, although it is also used in Phase 2 (see

Chapter 10 for more detail). This phase usually lasts about eight sessions, and you can expect to be eating regularly by the end of it. Reducing the restrictions you place on your diet should lower the number of times you binge eat and then purge. Often, even slight adjustments to the pattern of eating, such as adding a breakfast and mid-morning snack, result in an immediate decrease in bingeing and purging.

Phase 2: Identifying Binge Triggers

Whereas the general aims of Phase 1 continue to be implemented in the second phase of treatment, the focus shifts to learning how to identify and eliminate binge-eating triggers. During Phase 2, you will begin to identify the reasons for your binge episodes. You will be encouraged to broaden your food choices to decrease the number of foods you fear and avoid. If you did not learn formal problem-solving skills in Phase 1, you will be taught them as a general tool to accomplish the aims of Phase 2. These aims include helping you manage your negative moods, tolerate feelings of fullness, effectively deal with unstructured free time, and handle interpersonal interactions that may trigger your binges. You will learn to challenge problem thoughts concerning rigid food rules and your distorted views of your shape and weight. You will also begin to address the issues of negative body image. You will learn to revise problematic thinking patterns such as thinking in all-or-nothing terms. Finally, you will be assigned appropriate behavioral tasks consistent with these interventions, such as observing the shape and weight of other women to develop a more realistic notion of your own physical appearance. This phase will help you address and resolve some of the issues that underlie your problematic eating behaviors to increase the likelihood that the gains you make during treatment will be maintained.

Phase 3: Relapse Prevention

The last three sessions of treatment are usually devoted in part to a review and consolidation of the positive changes you have made during treatment. As you reflect upon the improvements in eating habits and associated behaviors and attitudes, you will also discuss strategies for maintaining and building upon these changes and anticipate any remaining problems. You will be encouraged to look ahead and create a plan of action to deal with future problems that can lead to lapses. At least some of these problems will already have been dealt with in Phase 2. Treatment culminates in the creation of a written maintenance or relapse-prevention plan that summarizes the most helpful aspects of the program and details strategies for getting back on track, should you experience a setback in your progress once treatment is completed. To allow more time for such residual problems to surface, it is suggested that the final three sessions be held at 2-week intervals.

Session Structure

Therapy proceeds more smoothly when the sessions are well structured. Each therapy session will be structured and well organized but will also offer some flexibility in the case of special concerns or issues that need to be addressed immediately. We've found that the 50-minute therapy hour can be used most productively when it follows consistent guidelines. Typically, your therapist will begin each session by asking you to provide a brief overview of areas of progress or difficulty since the last meeting. This will include a review of significant eating situations noted in your Daily Food Records (which will be introduced in the next chapter), such as episodes of restricting, bingeing, and purging, and attempts to change, whether successful or not. Since the treatment program is cumulative, in addition to the homework assigned in the previous session, you will be asked about your attempts to keep up with elements of the program that were introduced earlier. Depending on the record review, degree of progress, and phase of therapy, your therapist will then set a specific agenda for the remainder of the session, during which the main work of the session will occur. This will be followed by a review of the main points covered, which should naturally lead to a discussion of new topics and specific homework to be completed before the next session. This session agenda, although not carved in stone, does lend a degree of structure and organization to the sessions that is very helpful for most patients. Of course, should you have a crisis or emergency, you should ask your therapist for some airtime to address the relevant issues.

Therapy Session Structure

1. Brief overview of past week, using Daily Food Records as reference point

2. Detailed examination of Daily Food Records

3. Agenda setting by therapist, based on your overview of progress and problem situations

4. Introduction and discussion of new topics and interventions

5. Agreement upon homework assignments to be completed before the next session

6. Summary of learning, and wrap-up

Review of Self-Monitoring

After you check in with your therapist, you will turn to your completed Daily Food Records (See Chapter 3) and together review them in detail, first noting days on which your records were thorough, and then identifying any weaknesses, such as missing descriptions of quantities of food, food types, times of eating episodes, and so on. Next, the session will emphasize examining the problem eating patterns and situations noted that demonstrate a need for change. You can expect to be very thorough in discussing your food records. Your therapist will ask you to recreate in detail every episode of eating, including the time, type, and amount of food and liquid consumed; your perceptions of the episode as a meal, snack, or binge; your reasons for deciding to purge, if you did; and the situational factors, including specific thoughts and feelings, surrounding the eating episode. By asking you many questions about the thoughts and feelings you had during the eating episode, your therapist will attempt to elicit as much information as possible about your decision regarding your food intake in that particular instance, whether or not it involved binge eating and/or purging. As you progress through the program, you will become more active in initiating discussion of your Daily Food Records.

Is it common to feel uncomfortable about starting therapy?

It is not unusual in the initial stages of therapy to feel embarrassed or ashamed about sharing with your therapist such detailed information about your eating behavior—whether you are bulimic or a binge eater—because these behaviors may represent aspects of yourself that you have probably taken great pains to hide. Give it some time! Usually, the discomfort dissipates fairly quickly and is replaced by an array of positive feelings such as relief, hopefulness, and reassurance that you've found someone to support and assist you in your efforts to overcome your eating problems.

What if I have to miss a session?

We cannot overemphasize the importance of making treatment a top priority. This means not only working hard during and between sessions but also making a commitment to attend each one and to be on time unless it is absolutely impossible. On occasion, there may be unforeseeable circumstances that cause you to be late or even to miss your appointment altogether. It is important that you make every effort to avoid these circumstances! Lateness and spotty attendance may indicate a pessimistic attitude about the therapy (e.g., "It's not going to work anyway, so why even try?"). A less than full investment in your therapy *will* undermine its effectiveness by affecting your own sense of hopefulness about the therapy and the degree of collaboration between yourself and your therapist.

For the Binge-Eating Patient

If you are binge eating without purging, you will generally follow the same treatment guidelines and procedures as for bulimia, with a few additions and exceptions. First, the model for understanding the cycle of binge eating is slightly different from the one for bulimia nervosa. In bulimic patients, the role of dietary restriction is primary in triggering binge episodes. In binge eaters, low self-esteem, negative moods, and concerns about weight and shape are the most significant binge triggers. Moreover, when dietary restriction does precipitate binge episodes in binge-eating disorder, it appears in a slightly different form, that is, as a restrictive *mentality*. Most commonly, this mind-set is represented by constant "good intentions" to diet that are typically short-lived; large gaps between eating episodes that are substantial, if not excessive; and/or consumption of small amounts of high-calorie foods over long stretches of time (otherwise known as "binge grazing"). Whether bulimic or a binge eater, you stand to benefit tremendously from learning to structure and organize your meal plan to approximate the ideal of three meals and two snacks per day, eaten by the clock at regular intervals that are easily recognized as meal times. Implementing a meal plan of this nature will interrupt any form of chaotic and disorganized eating. In addition to the prescription to eat regularly, you will receive some general recommendations regarding food content and quantities, and exercise. You will be encouraged to adopt a "heart-smart" lifestyle that involves decreasing the amount of fat in your diet to no more than 30% of your total calories, controlling portion sizes, and maintaining a moderate regimen of exercise equivalent to walking 30 minutes per day. Interventions for binge-eating disorder are noted with an asterisk (*) in Table 2.1.

Table 2.1 Phases of Treatment

Phase 1: Behavior Change	Phase 2: Binge-Trigger Identification	Phase 3: Relapse Prevention
Regularly using Daily Food Records	Introducing "feared" or "off-limits" foods into the diet	Reviewing changes made in treatment
Implementing a regular meal pattern of 3 meals and 2 snacks per day	Identifying "risk factors" that precipitate binge episodes (low mood states, interpersonal conflicts, etc.)	Developing a written maintenance plan
Learning about weight and weighing oneself once per week	Challenging problem thoughts	Addressing remaining problem areas and anticipating future problems
Using alternative activities that compete with binge eating	Resolving problem situations	Devising a strategy for getting back on track following any setbacks
Controlling portion sizes*	Addressing weight and shape concerns and negative body image	
Decreasing fat intake*		
Undertaking a moderate regimen of exercise*		

*For the binge-eating patient

Summary

This chapter provided answers to some of your questions regarding the process of getting started in treatment. We also explored some concerns associated with starting treatment and presented a general program outline, including discussion of the treatment phases, specific interventions introduced in each phase, the structure of individual sessions, and the use and benefits of a treatment manual. The differences between the strategies for treating binge-eating disorder and for treating bulimia nervosa were outlined.

Homework

✎ Review Chapters 1 and 2 to strengthen your understanding of bulimia nervosa and binge-eating disorder and the structure and content of this treatment program.

Self-Assessment

Take some time to review the contents of this chapter and complete the following self-assessment. Answer by filling in the correct words or phrases. Answers can be found in the Appendix.

1. Describe the three phases of the program and list some of the interventions that are included in each phase.

   _____

   _____

   _____

   _____

2. What are some of the advantages of using a treatment manual?

   _____

   _____

   _____

   _____

3. Describe the general structure of your therapy session.

Chapter 3   *Learning More About Your Eating Pattern*

Goals

- To learn the importance of record keeping

- To become familiar with the Daily Food Record

- To learn about healthy weight and begin weighing yourself weekly

Review of Previous Chapter

You should now have a solid understanding of the nature of your eating disorder, the advantages and disadvantages of starting treatment at this time, the components of cognitive-behavioral therapy, and the benefits of using this workbook. You may review Chapters 1 and 2 if you have additional questions about your eating problems or the advisability of starting treatment at this time.

Overview

This chapter discusses the importance of maintaining Daily Food Records. Food records allow you to document your eating patterns and monitor problems, modifications, and improvements over time as you begin to apply the techniques learned in therapy. Maintaining food records is essential to your success in treatment. By recording your eating habits, you increase your awareness of both problem eating patterns and healthier eating patterns and the situational factors that contribute to each. This chapter presents the rationale for keeping records and includes pointers that can help you get the most out of your records. It also includes two sample completed Daily Food Records (shown in Figures 3.1 and 3.2) for you to use as models when filling out your own, a blank record for your use, and a discussion of the most common sources of hesitation regarding the use of food records.

You will also learn about healthy weight and how to establish a weekly weighing routine.

Why Keep Records?

The first step for successfully changing your problem eating behavior is to begin self-monitoring. Self-monitoring increases your awareness of your eating disorder and involves tracking the frequency, pattern, and "amount" of your problem eating behavior and also the factors (thoughts, feelings, or interpersonal interactions) associated with it. The most effective way of self-monitoring is to use a form called the Daily Food Record to document your food intake. Daily Food Records provide an ongoing source of documentation of all of your eating episodes, the types and quantities of the foods consumed at each episode, and the emotions and circumstances associated with it. It is important to complete this record as close to the time of eating as possible.

There are many advantages to keeping detailed records of your eating patterns. The first is that recording your eating behavior heightens your awareness of it. This applies to healthy *and* problem eating, including periods of restriction (skipping or skimping on meals or snacks) and episodes of binge eating, binge "grazing," or otherwise eating too much, or eating for emotional reasons. The most important aspects of your eating behavior to record in your Daily Food Record include the types and quantities of foods you ate, when you ate them, and the reasons for eating them. Reasons may include your level of hunger, specific cravings, the fact that it was mealtime, the occurrence of a stressful event, and so on. Over time, you will find that your detailed food records will help you and your therapist identify the situations and factors that contribute to healthy or more problematic eating episodes. By learning more about the factors that contribute to your binge episodes, you will begin to feel increasingly in control of your eating. You will eventually be able to anticipate high-risk situations and plan in advance to apply newly learned skills and strategies to improve your ability to cope with them.

Food records are considered the cornerstone of treatment. They enable you to identify patterns and recurring eating problems and to document and stay committed to your attempts to change. Food records can motivate you by providing an ongoing, written commentary about your progress over the course of a day or a week, or from the beginning to the end of treatment. You can refer to a partially completed record throughout the day to stay on track because, for example, it can put a given "overindulgence" into perspective. Referring to the Daily Food Record will help you counter any tendency toward exaggerated, negative perceptions of the type that can trigger additional binge eating episodes. It can also remind you that certain coping tools, such as some form of distraction, were helpful at an earlier point when you were tempted to overeat or binge. Over the long term, you can refer back to days', weeks', and months' worth of completed records to remind yourself of successful situations, and times when you could have done better. You can revisit the progress you've made and also use your food records to push yourself during periods of frustration or when you are lacking motivation. Finally, your completed food records are an excellent source of information for your therapist. He or she will ask you in detail about entries in your food records in order to better understand your eating problems. Your therapist will also refer to issues raised during the record review to focus the discussion in your sessions and to assign homework. Good record keeping, however, is not a simple exercise. It requires considerable time and energy and a strong commitment to convey the *real* picture of your eating behavior to yourself and your therapist. We will elaborate on the mechanics of good record keeping later in the chapter.

Common Concerns About Keeping Records

Despite the value and usefulness of keeping food records, it is not uncommon to be somewhat hesitant about self-monitoring.

Perhaps you have used food records previously and were unsuccessful. Even if prior attempts to record your eating were ineffective, we encourage you to give record keeping another chance! We expect that you will find food records helpful when used as part of this treatment because of the method and detail in which you and your therapist will examine them during your sessions. Also, reviewing your completed records with your therapist and consulting your personalized CBT model (see Chapter 4) will help you focus on the most relevant and important problem areas and devise clear-cut tactics for change.

Maybe you think that closer examination of your eating problems will only make matters worse. You may feel that you already spend too much time thinking about eating anyway. But there are many reasons for becoming *even more* vigilant about your eating, particularly when your goal is to improve it. As explained, the *process* of keeping track of your eating, and also the *product* of record keeping (a long-term food diary) can bring substantial benefits. When you monitor your own eating behavior, you become more aware of the context in which your eating problems occur, particularly the thoughts, feelings, and situations that place you at "high risk" for binge eating and purging. By noting the association between these types of factors and the occurrence of binge-eating episodes, you will be better able to identify and anticipate these difficult, triggering situations and to work out strategies for avoiding or responding differently to them. Retrospectively, you will be able to learn from past problems and successes with your eating by reviewing the contexts in which these types of eating episodes tended to occur and the coping strategies you attempted to implement. Noting long-term patterns will help you view your eating problems as more predictable and controllable.

The Importance of Timely Recording

Many individuals with bulimia or binge-eating disorder often acknowledge having a poor memory for the details of their binge episodes. They commonly describe "spacing out" while eating; even those who remain "aware" tend to reconstruct their eating patterns in a manner that reflects a global, overly negative, and black-and-white thinking style (e.g., overestimating the amount of food consumed, exaggerating its effect on their body weight and shape, viewing any departure from rigid rules about what should and should not be eaten as gross violations, and interpreting a small overindulgence as having "ruined" the whole day). For these reasons, we recommend that the most effective strategy for recording food intake is to do so *at the time of or as soon as possible after eating.* The advantages to this are considerable. First, the information obtained is most accurate and least vulnerable to distortion or poor memory. Second, the food record, when used in this fashion, can serve as a tool for planning meals and snacks in advance. When used in this way, the Daily Food Record can actually prevent or reduce the extent of overeating and purging by fostering a sense of commitment to sticking with a regular eating pattern and healthy food selections. Third, looking back over your records can help correct the types of perceptual distortions just described (e.g., the *sense* that you overate or "blew it," without actual data to support that feeling or impression). Reviewing your food record daily may help you stay focused on the positive, reminding you that you are still on track, even when you are ready to give up. Likewise, an accumulation of food records over time will provide data about your rate of progress and level of improvement during the course of treatment.

Daily Food Record Instructions

At first, writing down everything you eat may well be irritating and inconvenient, but soon it will become second nature and obviously valuable. We have yet to encounter anyone whose lifestyle makes monitoring truly impossible.

Use a new record (or records) each day, noting the date and day of the week in the space provided. Make entries as soon as possible after eating. It is too difficult to try to remember later what you ate or drank hours before.

You may photocopy the Daily Food Record on page 49 or download multiple copies from the Treatments *ThatWork*™ Web site at www .oup.com/us/ttw.

Column 1 of the Daily Food Record is for noting the time when you ate or drank anything during the day. Column 2 is for recording the type and amount of the food and liquid consumed. Do not record calories. Instead, provide a simple description of what you ate or drank. Remember that one of the two purposes of monitoring is to help you change. Obviously, if you are to record your food intake, you will have to carry your monitoring sheets with you. Meals should be put in parentheses. A meal may be defined as "a discrete episode of eating that was controlled, organized, and eaten in a "'normal'" fashion." List, but don't use parentheses for, snacks and other episodes of eating. Column 3 is for recording where you consumed the food or liquid. If you were in your home, identify the specific room. If you were at work, describe your exact location (e.g., sitting at your desk, in the cafeteria). Column 4 is for indicating whether you felt the particular eating episode was excessive and constituted a binge. Check the column if you considered it a binge. It is essential to record all the food you eat during any overeating episodes or binges. Column 5 is for recording when you vomit or take laxatives or water pills. If you have binge-eating disorder, you will use Column 5 to record any exercise you engaged in. Use Column 6 as a diary to record events or situations that influenced your eating. For example, if it seems that an argument might have precipitated a binge, you should make note of it in the column. You may wish to record other important events as well, even if they had no effect on your eating. It is also a good idea to write down any strong feelings, such as depression, anxiety, boredom, or loneliness, or feelings of "fatness" that you think might have contributed to your eating behavior. In addition, use Column 6 to record your weight each time you weigh yourself.

As previously stated, every session with your therapist will start with a review of your completed records. Remember to bring them with you each week.

Concerns About Weight Gain

You may be surprised to discover that eating regularly can help you overcome your problems with binge eating. In fact, the concept is counterintuitive for most bulimics and binge eaters, who typically think that *not eating*, rather than eating more, is the only way to overcome their eating disorder. Like others, you, too, might be con-

Time	Food and Liquid Consumed*	Location	Binge?	Purge?	Comments
8:00 am 11:15 am	1 cup Coffee, half a banana Nestle chocolate bar	Kitchen Desk			I was rushed Bought it a few days ago and left in my desk, bad but easy.
2:15 pm	Kraft Mac and Cheese Diet coke-half a can	Desk			Couldn't get out for lunch, not excessive eating but not good for me either
6:00 pm	2 wafer cookies with chocolate filling	Desk			
7:30 pm	4 KFC spicy breaded chicken strips, 1/4 cup of BBQ beans, 2 cups of corn with butter, 2 biscuits, ranch dressing, 1 pint of ice cream	In front of TV	Binge	Vomited	Had a quarrel with my boyfriend on the phone before this. Felt angry and resentful.

Figure 3.1 Example of Completed Daily Food Record for Bulimic Patient

vinced that eating more regularly can result only in a loss of control and automatic weight gain. In this session, you and your therapist will address your concerns about the possibility that you may gain weight as a result of this treatment program.

As previously mentioned, most studies of cognitive-behavioral therapies for bulimia nervosa have found either no weight gain or small gains of up to 4 lbs, usually in the form of water weight. Although the average weight gain may be misleading because some individuals will lose and others will gain weight during treatment, any weight change will tend to be in the direction of what is considered a more natural weight (e.g., if you began treatment below average in weight you will be more likely to gain into the normal range). This information should allay some of your fears that equate healthy eating with weight gain.

There are a couple of related points to consider. Bulimics often report some gastrointestinal distress and/or bloating when they first

Time	Food and Liquid Consumed*	Location	Binge?	Exercise	Comments
7:45 am	2 slices of bread with jam	kitchen		10 minute walk	A little hungry, just wanted to eat enough to last to lunch time
10:30 am	1 can Diet Pepsi				
11:30 am	8 thin mints, 2 cups of cheese nips, 3 pieces of pizza, 2 glasses of water	office	Binge		Started with the cookies, it's hopeless! I really don't like working here. I am out of control. I'll never lose weight
1:30 pm	15 Hershey's Kisses	office	Binge		Falling asleep, need sugar or something, don't want this, I'm not hungry
6:30 pm	2 thick peanut butter sandwiches, 2 glasses of milk				I want to stuff myself, out of control. I'm getting tired of this. I am alone.

Figure 3.2 Example of Completed Daily Food Record for Binge-Eating Patient

begin to experiment with eating more food and keeping it down. This discomfort is a normal and expected aspect of the recovery process for bulimics. After all, if you are bulimic, you've been denying your body the opportunity to digest and eliminate foods naturally for some time, so you need to practice and relearn formerly automatic processes. This can be very difficult—akin to learning to walk again after not using your legs for some time. In addition, many individuals with eating disorders can become overly sensitive to any indications of fullness, bloating, "fatness," or "constipation." You, like others, may think that the food you eat should "go through faster" and is "staying in your stomach too long." Even though the digestive processes in bulimic patients may slow down because of binge eating and vomiting habits, your expecting food to "pass right through" is unrealistic. If you do have frequent thoughts like this, you will have to work on tolerating feelings of fullness and normalizing the

Daily Food Record for Bulimic Patients

Time	Food and Liquid Consumed	Location	Binge?	Purge?	Comments

Daily Food Record for Binge-Eating Patients

Time	Food and Liquid Consumed	Location	Binge?	Exercise	Comments

sensation of having food in your stomach. We will return to this topic later.

For the Binge-Eating Patient

Those with binge-eating disorder will find that their weight usually stays the same or decreases somewhat as a result of treatment. Often, this happens in response to the binge eater's making food choices that represent a reduction in food intake; simultaneously, some binge eaters might begin to exercise, increasing their weight loss during the program.

Your therapist can provide some objective feedback regarding your weight and how it compares to the national average weight for your height. If you are overweight, you may be especially concerned about the possibility of further weight gain, especially if you feel as though you have been fighting a losing battle against weight all your life. Adopting a pattern of eating regular meals and snacks will help you develop healthy lifestyle habits to successfully manage your weight. Furthermore, when combined with a regular program of exercise and other weight-management strategies (e.g., decreasing fat intake), this program's recommendations can actually help you lose weight. Regularizing your eating can prevent binge episodes, thereby reducing the number of calories you consume. As illustrated by the cognitive-behavioral model of binge eating in Chapter 4, when you eat regularly, you are more satisfied and less inclined to give in to large, calorie-laden binges fueled by feelings of hunger and deprivation. For evidence to support this idea, just look around you. Many people are able to maintain a normal weight by eating regularly. It may be helpful for you to copy the healthy eating habits of people whose weights are normal. Observe their eating patterns, their portion sizes, and so on. It is essential that you try to normalize your eating habits.

Even after these words of encouragement, you may still feel discouraged and concerned about the potential for weight gain during treatment. In fact, those of you who have had a history of anorexia nervosa may demonstrate an even stronger tendency to experience anxious thoughts while you're engaged in treatment. You may have excessive worries and preoccupations with your body shape and weight. If you fall into this group, you should not be surprised if the process of normalizing your eating intensifies many of these fears and worries at first. Whenever these worries appear, however, it is important that you try as hard as you can to attribute them to the core irrational fears associated with your eating disorder. This means making the commitment to follow through with the recommended eating-behavior changes *despite* your feelings. Along with making these efforts, try as hard as you can to reassure yourself about your eating and your weight by reminding yourself that "it's going to be OK!" You can do this by referring to the factual information presented in this workbook. Interestingly enough, an accumulation of clinical experiences involving those with eating disorders suggests that individuals' body-weight and shape concerns tend to dissipate and their feelings about their bodies improve as they begin to eat more, in a more regular pattern, and stabilize their body weight in a healthier range (even when this might involve a small weight gain).

At the same time, it is important to point out that bulimic patients who begin treatment with extremely negative body images tend to show the poorest response to treatment. If you are someone who suffers from an extremely negative body image, you will need to work even harder than most. This will be especially true when you get to the portion of the treatment devoted to body-image issues. Your full commitment to treatment will be essential to challenge the negative thoughts and feelings you've had about your body and to develop alternative, more positive feelings (that can also motivate you to engage in healthier food behaviors). You might consider doing a cost–benefit analysis (using the worksheet provided in Chapter 1) to compare the ongoing costs of your bulimic behavior (e.g., shame and secrecy, money spent on food, time spent on the behavior, physical consequences such as damage to your teeth) with the benefits of ceasing the behavior (e.g., pride and relief at overcoming all of the above) even if minor weight gain or undesired shape changes occur. If you compare the benefits of successful treatment with those of no treatment long enough, you are likely to conclude that the costs of continuing to be bulimic are so substantial that it is nearly impossible to imagine a rationale for maintaining the bulimic behaviors, even if there is a remote possibility that these behaviors will help you maintain a lower weight.

Although we will address the issue of body-image concerns in more detail in Chapter 9, there are a couple of related points you should keep in mind at this early stage of treatment. First, your body weight will settle in where it should be—in its "natural" weight range—as you improve your eating habits. As you stop restricting your diet and start eliminating binge eating, purging, and compulsively exercising, your body will "thank you" by stabilizing its weight. Even if this body weight is higher than what you would ideally like to weigh, you have to trust and respect your body to gravitate toward a healthy and comfortable weight when it is treated well. Even better, this weight will be one that can be easily maintained because it is the right weight for you. We recommend that you consider accepting *just for now* the physiological realities of your body type, even if they include a higher than ideal body weight and/or sensitivities about certain aspects of your body shape. Accepting your weight and shape bodes well for treatment success and the long-term resolution of your eating problems.

Beginning a Healthy Weighing Routine

Part of accepting your body shape and weight involves adopting a healthy set of weighing behaviors. Eating-disordered individuals tend to adopt one of two patterns of weighing, best characterized as compulsive or avoidant. The compulsive types, who weigh themselves excessively, may step on the scale up to several times per day, often after meals and again after using the bathroom, setting themselves up to feel demoralized in response to normal and insignificant changes in weight. The avoidant types tend to avoid the scale altogether but seem to have some sense of their weight range and typically exaggerate changes in their weight following bouts of overeating or dieting. In either case, there is a heightened sensitivity to the importance and meaning of the numbers on the scale.

Realistically, everyone experiences daily weight fluctuations of up to a few pounds. A lot of the time, these changes are completely unrelated to the quantity of food you ate or the number of calories you consumed. Weight changes can be caused by shifts in the amount of fluid or bulk retained in the body, which may be related to the actual weight of the foods consumed and/or to the menstrual cycle. You may be surprised to learn that exercise can also increase your weight. Over-exertion can sometimes cause a buildup of fluids in the muscles, resulting in a short-lived increase in weight. Because of your eating disorder, you may exaggerate these minor shifts in weight and misinterpret them. You may assume they indicate an ongoing trend upward rather than a short-term "blip" that may very well be followed by a loss. The point is that changes in the numbers on the scale, which *everyone* experiences on a daily and weekly basis, do not necessarily equate to a real change in the amount of lean body mass or fat. In fact, we do not consider a weight change to be significant until we see a consistent trend in one direction for 4 consecutive weeks.

Establishing a Pattern of Weekly Weighing

To counteract the tendencies just described, we recommend that you adopt a pattern of regular but not too frequent weighing, such as weighing yourself once a week. The reasons for this are twofold. First, regular weighing will help you become desensitized to the numbers on the scale so you aren't scared or fearful of them. Second, it will allow you to obtain accurate data about changes in your body weight as you begin to improve your eating habits by decreasing binge eating and vomiting. After you weigh yourself, record your weight in the comments column of your Daily Food Record.

When considering setting up your weekly weighing regimen, take into account the following points. You should use the same scale and try to weigh yourself at the same time each week. It is best to weigh at a time when you can involve yourself in a structured activity immediately afterward so that you won't become preoccupied or overly focused on your weight. As with your episodes of eating, document your weight on your Daily Food Record, noting any thoughts, feelings, or behaviors associated with your weigh-in in the comments column.

Summary

The first step in attempting to change a problem eating behavior involves increasing your awareness of it through regular and accurate record keeping. Keeping detailed Daily Food Records, including information about what and how much you've eaten and the situational factors that affected your eating is essential to your success in this treatment program. Food records will provide the information you and your therapist need to help you change your problem eating patterns. You will review your records in detail during each therapy session, and the problem areas identified through your entries will provide the focus for discussion and homework assignments. Although you may have some second thoughts about using food records, the methods for using and reviewing the records suggested here ensure that the advantages will exceed any perceived costs.

In addition to covering record keeping, we introduced in this chapter the concept of a "natural weight" that is defended by your body when it's being treated well and discussed commonly held fears regarding weight gain secondary to establishing a regular pattern of eating.

Before going on to the next chapter, reread and review the material just presented.

Homework

✎ Complete the Daily Food Records for the remainder of today and every day until your next therapy session.

✎ Establish a regular weighing regimen. Decide on a time and place, and make a plan as to what you will do after weighing yourself.

✎ Record your weight for the week and write down any associated thoughts or feelings in the comments column of your Daily Food Record.

Take some time to review the contents of this chapter and complete the following self-assessment. Answer by filling in the correct words or phrases, or by circling T (True) or F (False). Answers can be found in the Appendix.

1. What is the first step to change a problem behavior?

    _____

    _____

    _____

    _____

2. Name some of the ways in which Daily Food Records can be helpful in the treatment of bulimia and binge-eating disorder.

    _____

    _____

    _____

    _____

3. To be most effective, Daily Food Record entries should be made (when) _____ in relation to the eating episode in question.

4. What types of information do Daily Food Records contain about eating episodes?

    _____

    _____

    _____

    _____

5. Describe the concept of natural weight.

_____

_____

_____

_____

6. Describe the rationale for once-weekly weighing.

_____

_____

_____

_____

7. Everyone experiences fluctuations in their weight
    for a variety of reasons that may not be related to
    actual weight gain.   T   F

Chapter 4

Understanding the Binge-Eating Cycle

Goals

     ■ To review the model for understanding bulimia nervosa and binge-eating disorder

     ■ To work with your therapist to apply the model to your own eating disorder

     ■ To discuss self-induced vomiting and laxative abuse and understand why they don't really rid your body of calories

     ■ To learn to engage in pleasurable alternative activities instead of eating

Review of Previous Chapter

Since the last session, you should have completed at least one week of Daily Food Records. Make sure to use the comments column of your food record to note the situational factors that may be linked to your eating, such as your hunger level, thoughts, feelings, or interpersonal interactions. Make sure to congratulate yourself on beginning to regularly self-monitor your eating behaviors. Self-monitoring is a necessary first step in the behavior-change process. By examining your records in detail, you will learn more about the specifics of your eating patterns. If you have any questions about self-monitoring, raise these questions with your therapist and review the previous chapter before going on.

Overview

This chapter reviews the model for understanding bulimia nervosa and binge-eating disorder and discusses it in more detail. The model identifies strict dieting, low self-esteem, concerns about shape and weight, and negative mood as the factors that contribute most significantly to binge eating in bulimia nervosa and binge-eating disorder. Whatever the nature of your eating disorder, your therapist will work with you to tailor the model so that it applies to your unique struggle. Then, based on the model, your therapist will prescribe a regular and structured eating pattern similar to three meals and two snacks a day, eaten by the clock. An organized meal plan like that recommended here will assist you in reestablishing regular eating habits and normal feelings of hunger and fullness that may have been disrupted during the time you've had an eating disorder. Finally, the chapter will discuss the importance of engaging in pleasurable alternative activities incompatible with eating and taking steps to control the number of inappropriate situations with which you associate eating to better control your urges to eat.

A Model for Understanding the Binge-Eating Cycle

As you begin to collect completed Daily Food Records, you may notice patterns in the occurrence of problematic eating and/or purging. The patterns most likely reflect aspects of the cognitive-behavioral model of bulimia and binge-eating disorder, and your food records will help you by illustrating which aspects of the model are contributing the most to your eating problems. The CBT model suggests that binge eating is affected by the interrelationship of several factors, including calorie restriction, concerns about weight and shape, low self-esteem, and negative mood. The model can be applied to both bulimia nervosa and binge-eating disorder.

The Model Applied to Bulimia Nervosa

For those of you who are binge eating and purging, the model suggests that strict dieting (usually driven by weight and shape concerns) is one of the most significant triggers of binge-eating episodes. Dieting is associated with reducing the number of eating episodes and restricting the variety and quantity of foods eaten, and is accompanied by rules about what one should and shouldn't eat, possibly even extending to the times of day that certain types or quantities of foods are acceptable. Like others with eating disorders, you may have started to diet after a real or perceived weight gain, after exposure to some form of stress, or in an attempt to improve a negative or depressed mood. Regardless of the reason, dieting or purging creates a state of physical and psychological deprivation. Ultimately, this state of deprivation undermines your resolve to continue dieting because the only way to reverse it is by eating. When you are deprived, control breaks down and you may gravitate toward foods forbidden by the rules of your diet. The enjoyment of eating these foods, combined with the guilt over breaking food rules, may set up a vicious cycle of additional dieting and binge eating. Dieting thereby increases the risk for out-of-control binge eating. Binges might be thought of most straightforwardly as the way your body responds to dieting and purging, overriding a strict undereating and/or purging pattern and making up for the lost calories. Seen in this light, binge eating can be considered a natural reflex that occurs in response to the deprivation state dieting causes.

Compounding the problem of binge eating is disruption of the normal sensations of hunger and fullness. After dealing with an eating disorder like bulimia, you may feel hungry all day because of the caloric deficit you've created by dieting. In persons without eating disorders, hunger usually occurs before mealtime and does not last all day long. Alternatively, you may never feel hungry, even after going several hours without food. The experience of satiety or fullness is disrupted by greatly varied meal sizes, ongoing efforts to restrict your diet, episodes of binge eating and purging, and, in general, trying to control your appetite with your mind rather than relying more naturally on your gut. You may notice that you feel full after taking in only a small amount of food. Or, you may feel full only after eating very large amounts of food. In any case, by this point, you probably feel unable to rely on and trust your internal cues of hunger and fullness to regulate your eating. This lack of predictability contributes to a pattern of alternating between overly controlled dieting and out-of-control bingeing.

The Model Applied to Binge-Eating Disorder

If you are binge eating without purging, your experience of restriction may be somewhat different, characterized by strong *intentions* to diet (along with an internal set of ideals or rules regarding what and how much you should or should not eat), large gaps between meals or snacks, and/or a pattern of eating very small and generally unsatisfying snacks ("grazing") throughout the day. Although mild restriction may be present, your overeating episodes probably are not triggered primarily by dietary deprivation or hunger. Rather, if you are binge eating without purging, you are more likely to be regularly *overeating* rather than *undereating*. This means you are taking in *more* calories than you actually need. Factors other than dietary restriction, such as negative moods, low self-esteem, and/or your ongoing concerns about your weight, your shape, and your suboptimal eating behaviors probably play a more important role in triggering your binges.

Bingeing

Whether or not you are purging, your binges may be large (up to several thousand calories in one sitting) or relatively small. Binges of bulimics tend to be larger than those of binge eaters. If you are bulimic, you may be driven to large binges because of the extreme hunger you feel as a result of dietary restriction, and the fact that you are also purging. On the other hand, binges also seem to be subjective, or "in the eyes of the beholder," in the sense that a binge is also commonly accompanied by a feeling of being "out of control." In certain instances, this feeling may be based on the experience of having violated particular rules related to food contents or quantities, or the timing of an eating episode. Following a binge, it is common for the individual to feel physical and emotional discomfort associated with actual fullness or the perception of having broken "food rules."

Purging

Purging is an attempt to compensate for a binge episode by eliminating food from the body. In the short term, all forms of purging, including vomiting, starving, compulsively exercising, and using laxatives, water pills, or substances that cause vomiting, like ipecac, seem to decrease the uncomfortable feelings of fullness and reduce the fears of weight gain associated with a binge. Purging provides the illusion that you will not absorb any of the ingested calories and will avoid weight gain. Purging becomes associated with a range of positive emotions such as anxiety reduction, relief, relaxation, exhilaration, and a sense of "purity" from experiencing a catharsis of bad feelings. In the long term, however, purging seems to intensify negative thoughts and feelings about oneself and one's body shape and weight. Depression, guilt, and a sense of being out of control and ineffective may also follow a purge episode. Typically, the negative feelings that follow either a binge or a purge episode (after the initial exhilaration of eating or relief at getting the excess food out of one's system) tend to be interpreted through the lens of the eating disorder. They are seen as pertaining primarily to one's dissatisfaction with weight and shape rather than to disgust with again lapsing into a binge-and-purge cycle.

Although it affords short-term relief from the discomfort of overeating, purging may result in adverse physical effects, such as weakness, dizziness, exhaustion, and dehydration.

Interrupting the Cycle of Binge Eating

Based on the cognitive-behavioral model of bulimia, the first step to interrupting the binge-eating cycle is to establish a regular pattern of meals and snacks. Nevertheless, questions may arise as you consider making fairly radical changes to your current eating pattern.

For example, you may be inclined to ask how it is that eating more can help you solve your problem with binge eating. Given the recommendation to eat more, the cognitive-behavioral model of binge eating may be at odds with your view of your eating problems and the strategies you need to implement to overcome them. Like other bulimics, you may believe that the only way to control your binges is to adhere to a very strict diet or to stop eating altogether. Eating more is probably the last thing you would ever consider as a potentially helpful strategy. But obviously your attempts to control your eating through dieting have not been altogether successful. *In order to overcome binge eating, you need to eat more, not less.* But just eating more is not enough. Rather, meals and snacks must be consumed in a structured, organized, controlled, and *satisfying* manner. Once you establish a structured pattern of eating, your feelings of hunger will decrease and you will begin to experience more positive thoughts as you gain control of your eating habits. In turn, you will binge less frequently. The following reasons clarify the rationale behind this.

Dieting and Deprivation

Dieting results in a state of deprivation that affects you physiologically and psychologically and increases the likelihood that you will binge. Even if you tend to label your eating habits as "healthy" or "low-fat," endorsement of any of the following behaviors suggests that you are engaging in some form of dieting. *Purging* has an effect similar to dieting in that it depletes your energy stores and contributes to a feeling of deprivation.

Types of Dieting

- Limiting the overall amount of calories consumed

- Decreasing or eliminating certain foods or food groups (e.g., cookies, pizza, or fats and sugars)

- Reducing the number of eating episodes per day

- Relying on a series of extensive rules about what, when, and how much you should or shouldn't eat

Loss of Control

Deprivation leads to loss of control over food. Each one of the dieting behaviors listed represents an intention to control rather than satisfy your appetite, and this results in a sense of physical and psychological deprivation. Prolonged deprivation has the effect of breaking down your control, particularly with respect to forbidden foods. You may hear an internal dialogue such as the following: "I shouldn't have that piece of cake. But that's not fair! Other people get to eat cake and I want some now!" When you are hungry and deprived, you are more likely to give in to the urge to eat cake, or any other "off-limits" food, in even larger than usual quantities.

Regular Eating Increases Your Control

Regular eating does not cause weight gain. Rather, it facilitates long-term weight management. The results of most of the cognitive-behavioral treatment studies suggest that, on average, patients gain 0–4 lbs while in treatment. This weight gain usually represents weight "correction," a gain into a more natural range, especially for underweight individuals. Although it may initially sound counterintuitive, the fact of the matter is that eating regularly is one of the most effective strategies for weight management. As we just discussed, as you begin to eat more food more regularly, your desire to binge will diminish. And when binge eating decreases, your overall caloric intake also decreases. Studies have found that in many bulimics who are maintaining their weight, the amount of calories ingested, purged, and retained during a day is about equivalent to that taken in by an average, weight-maintaining person eating regular meals and snacks. This suggests that the binges serve the purpose of making up for the caloric deficit caused by missing or skipping meals. So, instead of bingeing, you might as well consume the calories through regular, healthful eating. It's a far more satisfying and effective way to manage your weight over the long haul. Research on weight changes in abstinent and non-abstinent binge eaters following cognitive-behavioral weight-loss treatment shows that bingeing contributes to weight gain, whereas abstinence from binge eating corresponds to weight loss (see graph in Figure 4.1).

Regular Eating Improves Self-Esteem and Mood

An organized and structured approach to eating can improve self-esteem and counteract low-mood states. In addition to eating in response to hunger and deprivation, binge eaters binge in response to low moods and negative feelings about themselves. Although binge eating might provide temporary relief or distraction from troubling feelings, it actually contributes to a worsening of mood and self-esteem, which leads to further binge eating. An organized and structured meal pattern prevents the emergence of negative feelings following problematic eating episodes (e.g., binges) and also decreases the likelihood that food will be selected as the primary means to gratify, soothe, and comfort oneself when one is experiencing emotional difficulties.

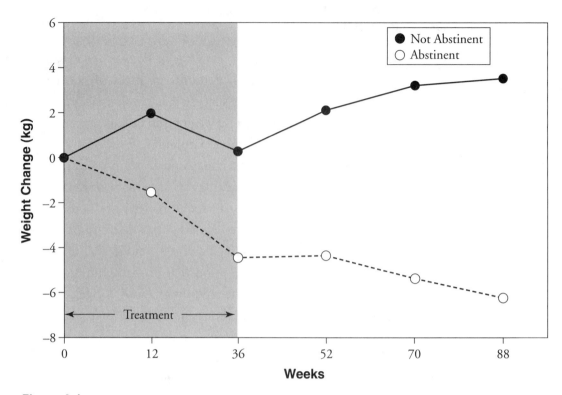

Figure 4.1 Weight Change in Clients with Binge-Eating Disorder

The cognitive-behavioral model goes a long way toward helping you understand how you become "stuck" in the cycle of binge eating and purging. When you diet or purge, you deprive yourself of food and energy. Then, when confronted with appetizing food, you experience an overwhelming urge to compensate for your lack of energy. When your control breaks down and you eat foods that your diet forbids, your enjoyment of eating these foods, combined with guilt about breaking food rules, sets up a vicious cycle of further dieting and binge eating. Similarly, in binge-eating disorder, negative feelings may lead you to binge, and the guilt that results may lead to more negative feelings and to intentions to diet, both of which lead to more bingeing. The model, whether applied to bulimia or binge-eating disorder, portrays the cycle of binge eating as a *behavioral problem* involving restrictive dieting and negative feelings, not a matter of character. The model lends itself to straightforward interventions that are effective in interrupting the cycle of binge eating, including the initial prescription to eat more regularly and to discontinue purgatives.

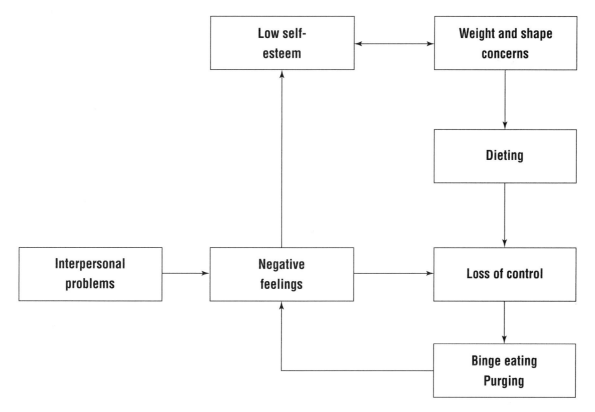

Figure 4.2 A Model of Factors Maintaining Binge Eating and Purging

A graphic representation of the cognitive-behavioral model for understanding binge eating is shown in Figure 4.2.

Sue's Model

Remember Sue from the case study in Chapter 1? Based on the model presented, let's take a look at the factors contributing to the onset and maintenance of her eating disorder.

1. Sue was an overweight, unhappy child whose eating was constantly monitored and who was encouraged by her mother to diet unhealthfully from a very young age. She had led an active social life as a teen and young adult, but after having her two children, she began to doubt herself as a woman and sought extreme weight loss as a means to find meaning and value and achieve perfection.

2. Sue joined a commercial diet program to achieve significant weight loss, and her dieting efforts were restrictive and included strenuous exercise. Eventually, she also started to purge, particularly after episodes of perceived overeating, and her purging techniques included vomiting, taking water pills, fasting, and exercising rigorously.

3. These forms of purging had the unintended effect of increasing the intensity of Sue's hunger. In addition, the more Sue purged, the more she binged, and vice versa. As this vicious cycle continued, she began to feel more and more out of control.

4. The people around her, who began to notice her fatigued and rundown appearance, confronted Sue about her disordered eating behaviors. Only then was she motivated to enter a treatment program, which proved to be beneficial only in the short term, before she relapsed.

5. Sue began her second round of treatment after taking a medical disability leave from work. She was at a point at which she could no longer tolerate the accumulation of negative feelings about herself. She felt out of control, fat, ugly, and lazy. She felt physically ill most of the time because of the ingrained nature of her restrict, binge, and purge behaviors, and she was genuinely worried about her health on all levels.

Based on the model, take a moment to describe the manner in which the specific factors of mood, self-esteem, dietary restriction, and purging have contributed to the onset and maintenance of your problem with binge eating. Use the space provided.

Factors that Contribute to Binge Eating

_____

_____

_____

_____

_____

The therapeutic interventions offered here are designed to interrupt the self-perpetuating nature of the binge-eating cycle. If you can understand and believe in this model as an explanation for your eating disorder, the place to start should be fairly obvious, even if somewhat difficult. It involves altering your pattern of eating by eliminating strict dieting. To accomplish this, your first assignment is to establish a regular pattern of eating, including three meals and two snacks per day eaten at specific times. Your therapist will work with you to tailor this prescription so that it fits into your lifestyle (e.g., if you work nights, or in any other way maintain an inconsistent daily schedule) and so that the interventions are useful and relevant, given the exact nature of your eating problems. For example, you and your therapist will discuss the ways that your eating is affected by different types of days and varying schedules (e.g., weekdays, weekends, business trips, vacations). Also, you will examine the various types of eating situations that you encounter (e.g., home alone, at a restaurant with friends). Changes in your schedule and the availability of foods will also be discussed to determine their influence on all aspects of your eating disorder. Your therapist will assist you in taking small steps toward change, starting first with the changes that are easiest to make and then progressing to those that are more difficult for you.

Eating Style and Stimulus Control

You will also be encouraged to use the comments column of your Daily Food Record to take note of your eating style. For example, you may tend to eat ice cream from the container while standing up, eat breakfast in the car on the way to work, or snack on cookies in bed. The rationale for addressing these issues is that as you learn to pay attention to the context in which you are eating and to limit your eating to appropriate places (e.g., at the kitchen table, in a restaurant) you will slowly reestablish habits that enhance your sense of mastery and control over eating. It is helpful to think about stimulus control and how to break the links between situations that should not involve eating and the act of eating. For example, if you break a pattern of eating in the car or in bed, those situations will no longer provide cues to eat, whereas the association between eating while sitting at the table will be strengthened if you continue to eat your meals and snacks only while seated. Also, it is important to "binge proof" your home, to the extent possible, by stocking up on healthy foods you can eat in reasonable portions at scheduled meal and snack times and eliminating large stocks of foods known to trigger your binges.

Managing your eating patterns also involves identifying and then eliminating eating in situations or locations that should not naturally include food. For example, you shouldn't eat in your car or at your desk, or while working at your computer, reading in bed, or taking a bath. Each time you eat in one of these situations or places that are inherently not related to eating, you strengthen an association between that situation or place and the act of eating. Eventually, you may want food whenever you find yourself in similar situations or places, even though you aren't necessarily hungry. To break these associations between "food-inappropriate" situations and eating, you need to learn to limit your eating to traditional settings, like the kitchen or dining room table or breakfast bar. Taking control of your eating also involves learning to make good choices about what you purchase when you're at the grocery store. First and foremost, it is important to avoid grocery shopping when you are hungry. Entering a grocery store, especially a large one with lots of tempting foods, can be over-stimulating to the taste buds when your stomach is already growling because you have been restricting your diet. Realistically, even if you are not hungry when you go grocery shopping, the situation is high risk because of your eating disorder. It is a good idea to always go grocery shopping with a list in hand. This prevents you from buying nonessential treats or goodies that may trigger a binge. You might even choose to go grocery shopping with a friend or significant other, just to make sure there is an "external control" in place (not that you need to tell them that this is the reason you're asking them to join you)! Avoid purchasing large amounts of trigger or problem foods that you intend to store at home. Instead, your grocery list should include relatively healthy (not just diet!) foods that can help you succeed with (and enjoy) your plan of eating three meals and two snacks a day. You might also consider purchasing prepackaged foods to make portion control easier for you, particularly if you are packing meals to take with you to work.